FOR

I THINK YOU'D ENJOY THIS BOOK BECAUSE

FROM

PRINCIPLES FOR THE NEXT CENTURY OF WORK

Sense & Respond Press publishes short, beautiful, actionable books on topics related to innovation, digital transformation, product management, and design. Our readers are smart, busy, practical innovators. Our authors are experts working in the fields they write about.

The goal of every book in our series is to solve a real-world problem for our readers. Whether that be understanding a complex and emerging topic, or something as concrete (and difficult) as hiring innovation leaders, our books help working professionals get better at their jobs, quickly.

Jeff Gothelf & Josh Seiden

Series co-editors **Jeff Gothelf** and **Josh Seiden** wrote *Lean UX* (O'Reilly) and *Sense & Respond* (Harvard Business Review Press) together. They were co-founding Principals of Neo Innovation (sold to Pivotal Labs) in New York City and helped build it into one of the most recognized brands in modern product strategy, development, and design. In 2017 they were short-listed for the Thinkers50 award for their contributions to innovation leadership. Learn more about Jeff and Josh at www.jeffgothelf.com and www.joshseiden.com.

The Invisible Leader
*Facilitation secrets for catalyzing change,
cultivating innovation, and commanding results*
Elena Astilleros

The Government Fix
How to innovate in government
Hana Schank & Sara Hudson

Outcomes Over Output
Why customer behavior is the key metric for business success
Josh Seiden

What CEOs Need to Know About Design
A business leader's guide to working with designers
Audrey Crane

To keep up with new releases or submit book ideas to the press
check out our website at www.senseandrespondpress.com

Issued in print and electronic formats.

ISBN 979-8-6331415-1-1 (KDP paperback)

Designer: Mimi O Chun
Interior typesetting: Jennifer Blais

Published in the United States by Sense & Respond Press

Printed and bound in the United States.

1 2 3 4   23 22 21 20

Natalija Hellesoe & Sonja Mewes

OKRs AT THE CENTER

How to use goals to drive ongoing change
and create the organization you want

SENSE &
RESPOND
PRESS

INTRODUCTION

Companies today are using OKRs—Objectives and Key Results—to improve the way they set and work with goals.

Along the way, they discover something else: To really improve the way you work with goals implies you have to make other changes. Changes in how you plan work. Changes in how you lead people or people lead themselves. Changes in how you make decisions. Changes in how you reward people. Changes in how you budget. Changes on a personal, an interpersonal, and an organizational level.

In short, if you really, sincerely start pursuing goal-setting in a new way, you will discover that **goals live at the center** of everything you do. What's exciting about this is where it leads: Changing how you work with goals has the potential to drive ongoing change and bring new ways of working to the whole organization.

That's what this book is about: how goals live at the center of your organizational system and how you can leverage their potential for organizational development by adopting OKRs in an intentional way.

CHAPTER 1: DRIVING CHANGE WITH OKRs

Claire Williams is the CEO of Innovio, a successful innovation and marketing agency based in Germany that's been in business for 15 years. Like many CEOs today, Claire and her management team are trying to change the way their company works in order to meet the demands of today's business environment:

*"We work in a very competitive and fast-paced market,
and our clients have high expectations. Right now,
growth is the highest priority for our firm—we've hired
many people, and have to grow our business to keep
the lights on. At the same time, we see competitors and
market changes. We need to adopt new ways of working
to future-proof the firm."*

Today Innovio has 500 employees, distributed across five offices
in Europe. Over the last few years, the company has started to
implement some new ways of working.

*"We've experimented a little with agile project
management, but there's so much more we need to
improve—sometimes it is hard to decide where to
start and what to do first. So now we are looking for
other concepts and tools to help us in this important
transition."*

When Peter Schmidt joined Innovio as the new head of human
resources, his highest priorities were understanding the current
situation and discovering potential areas of improvement. His first
step was fact-finding, so he set out to interview some colleagues.
He was especially interested in how the company works with goals,
but wanted to understand challenges beyond that as well.

Peter spoke to different people, but he heard many similar
stories. There was lots of good news. People really like working
at Innovio because they appreciate the diverse projects and their
colleagues. Many have worked with the same clients for years and
enjoyed these relationships as well.

Peter heard about problems though, too: Innovio had taken
on many new clients in order to drive growth. As a result, people

were spread thin: External and internal projects were piling up. People were having a hard time keeping up with client needs, and the company was struggling to compete with the new innovations appearing in the market. Added to that, people felt that priorities were often unclear or worse—they kept changing in response to short-term client requests and new initiatives driven by the management team. Alignment was also a challenge: Sometimes the goals of different teams seemed to conflict—like when sales would promise things to clients that were not aligned with the vision and strategy of the product teams. And above all, Peter learned that though there is a company-wide roadmap for major initiatives, nobody can remember the last time an initiative was completed on time.

UNCERTAINTY AND COMPLEXITY DEMAND NEW PERSPECTIVES

Does this sound familiar to you? It probably does since many companies face these kinds of challenges. And though Innovio is not a real company (we've created this and other cases to represent many of the companies we've worked with and learned from over the years), we hope the stories we're sharing reflect some of your own experiences.

Organizations today face a world of accelerated change, highly personalized customer needs, a growing demand for purpose and belonging, and disruptive competitors. They are surrounded by a world of fast-developing technological innovation. In this complex world, no single expert or manager can foresee the future or manage all dependencies and possibilities. Companies need new habits, structures, and processes that enable new ways of working everywhere in the organizational system and for all employees.

The search for ways to address these trends has many labels. Whether you call it "transformation" or "new ways of working," you'll see many companies engaged in trying to adopt new practices and shed older methods that no longer serve their needs. In our experience, companies that are seeking to change the way they work tend to be seeking a set of benefits and improvements that fall into six important themes, or principles:

» To create strong **focus**
» To foster better **alignment**
» To drive **value-creation**
» To increase **meaningful contribution**
» To enable **autonomous decision-making**
» To embed **fast learning cycles**

Companies that embark on transformational journeys tend to be trying to embed these principles into their DNA. These are lofty goals though, and changes like these take time—and change is never a linear process. Developing yourself, your team, or your organization is a never-ending process. It requires courageous decision-making, persistence, a high degree of self-awareness, and the ability to understand and react to the challenges, hurdles, and setbacks that arise in the process. But it can lead to great rewards.

For these reasons, it helps to have a driver—something to act as a forcing function, or a pulse—that will help you start, and help you sustain momentum when you meet the inevitable challenges. We believe that OKRs can be this driver.

DRIVING CHANGE WITH A DIFFERENT WAY OF WORKING WITH GOALS

W. Edwards Deming famously claimed that 95% of the variation in the performance of an organizational system is caused by the system itself, while only 5% is caused by the people. If this is true, then the most effective way to change an organization is to focus on changing the system.

Your organization is a complex system, shaped by its people. An organizational system is made of many interlinked elements: purpose and vision, values and norms, structures and processes, the design of compensation and benefits, and so much more. Together these elements shape and reflect your culture. And they have a major influence on organizational success—no matter how you define success, whether that's shareholder value or manifesting your company purpose.

"OKRs AT THE CENTER" MODEL

When you imagine a complex system, it can be helpful to think of it as a living, constantly evolving organism rather than a mechanically running machine. With a machine, you can simply swap parts, but with an organism, every part influences every other part. This is true for system-wide forces as well as team-specific ways of working. And this means that, while goals are an essential part of the organizational ecosystem, they don't stand alone.

Instead, we think of goals as an essential cornerstone of any organizational system—that's what the "OKRs at the Center" model above means—because they represent what both the whole organization and all of its parts are trying to achieve. They influence (and are influenced by) our decision-making, our organizational structures, our compensation—everything! Consequently, all organizational elements and their transformation are connected to the way you set goals. You can't change these elements independently.

And most important, for this conversation, you can't successfully change the way you set goals without changing other parts of the system as well. Instead you'll find that achieving your desired benefits will mean you'll need to make changes elsewhere—to your strategy, to your organizational structure, perhaps to compensation, and maybe even to your values and norms. These changes will take courage, but they are critical to success. That's why we see goals at the center of every organizational transformation.

When you change the way you work with goals, it changes the way you work together across the whole organizational system. It has the potential to deliver tremendous benefits—if you dare to make courageous decisions along the way.

GET MOVING WITH OKRs

Back at Innovio, Peter, the new head of HR, began reaching out to former colleagues and friends to collect new ideas about what could help them succeed. When attending a "Future of Work" conference to get more inspiration, he stumbled upon the concept of OKRs, a goal-setting approach he had only briefly heard about before.

OKRs are often associated with Google, but the idea was originally developed in the 1970s at Intel by Andy Grove. At the time, Intel was trying to shift the whole company strategy and transform itself into a world-class microprocessor supplier in a very short time frame. To succeed, Intel would need to refocus.

Grove's system helped the company focus on a quarterly north star—the **Objective**. This objective was accompanied by a specific set of measurable **Key Results** to quantify it and allow people to understand progress toward the objective.

Google was introduced to OKRs in 1999, when former Intel employee John Doerr introduced the system to the management team at the young company. Google has worked with OKRs ever since. Through employees of these companies, the concept has spread throughout Silicon Valley, the tech industry, and beyond. If you want to read more about the history, see *Measure What Matters* by John Doerr. (This and other references can be found in the Reading List at the end of this book.)

At the conference, Peter was impressed by the success stories he heard about OKRs. He especially liked the benefits mentioned: better alignment, clearer focus, continuous learning, and autonomous decision-making in teams. Reflecting on the interviews he had conducted at Innovio and considering the current challenges at the company, he was hooked and began looking into the details of OKRs.

OKRs IN A NUTSHELL

So how do OKRs work?

Goals begin with Purpose, Mission, and Vision. These describe the company's long-term goals and its reason for existence. They help articulate meaning, and give people a general orientation. As inspiring and important as they are though, they are too high-level to help prioritize the initiatives and day-to-day challenges that every employee faces. If you worked for Microsoft in the 1980s and looked only at the company vision—"A computer on every desk and in every home"—would you have known exactly which initiative to drive next?

This is where the concept of OKRs steps in: **OKRs bridge the gap between the high-level purpose or vision and the specific tasks needed to make it a reality. OKRs describes the next ambitious and inspiring step you want to take in order to achieve the high-level goals.**

Similar to a microstrategy, the Objective describes the next step toward the company's purpose or vision. OKRs work on a shorter timeline than Vision, and are oriented around using the most current information you can gather. So, after you complete an Objective, you pause, reflect, and calibrate the next step with the latest information available at that point in time so that—step by step—you can get closer to what you are trying to achieve.

As much as Objectives provide direction, there is still a lot of room for misinterpretation and contrary activities in pursuit of the Objective. *What's the best way to achieve this Objective? How do we know that we're on the right track?*

This is where the second part of OKRs come in—the Key Results. Key Results quantify the Objective with measurement criteria so you know whether or not you are on track—and know when you have actually achieved your Objective.

They also allow you to build a more holistic picture of the Objective, because different Key Results can mirror different aspects of the Objective. You can consider quality, satisfaction, performance, usage, sales, collaboration, and so on.

OKRs IN A NUTSHELL

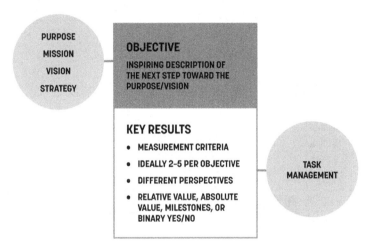

What do we mean by that? Imagine your favorite coffee cup for tea or coffee. To paint a picture of your cup, you would need to turn it in your hands, look at its surface area, inside and outside, top and bottom, and probably knock on it to test its material. To fully describe it, you would need to look at it from many different angles. **To get an overall picture of your Objective, you need to look at the different aspects of it the same way you look at your cup. You then express these different aspects as measurable Key Results.**

In this book, we will use "OKRs" to describe the concept and "OKR Set" to describe a specific goal consisting of one Objective and various Key Results.

THE OKR CYCLE

The way you define your OKR Sets—how you express your goals and make them measurable—is only one part of the OKR concept. Another critical part of OKRs is the ongoing process of using them. This is called the "OKR Cycle." The OKR Cycle refers to the entire process from OKR Definition and Alignment to the regular OKR Check-ins you hold during the cycle, and finally to the OKR Reflection at the end of each cycle.

A typical OKR Cycle looks like this:

OBJECTIVES AND KEY RESULTS CYCLE

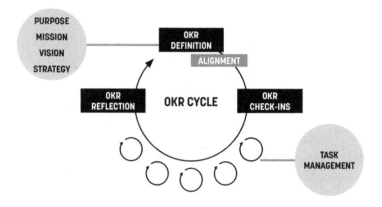

OKRs are typically **defined** for a short time period, often for a single quarter. They are based, as we said, on the company's purpose, vision, and mission, but also on the current strategy of the company.

The definition is followed by an **alignment** process to link all company levels and different teams. Alignment can be executed top-down, bottom-up, or with a mix of both. The result is aligned OKR Sets for the whole company, which are, ideally, transparent to all employees.

Following this, you begin a rhythm of **OKR Check-ins**, which allow teams to track progress on a regular (e.g., weekly) basis to change tactics as needed and remove obstacles along the way.

Finally, an **OKR Reflection** at the end of each OKR Cycle provides insights that you can use to improve the OKR Process and to define your OKR Sets for the next period. The reflection provides critical feedback on your method of working with goals and how your company approaches its challenges. It helps you learn about your culture and how you collaborate. It also provides insights on the potential for improvement of other organizational elements, which is why we say that OKRs can be the driver of organizational change. The rhythm provided by this regular cycle of planning, execution, and reflection can be a motor that drives your change efforts.

So, to summarize, the OKR Cycle is an iterative process that allows you to define ambitious and measurable goals in an aligned, participatory, and transparent way. From there, you work with these goals through a process of regular check-ins and reflections.

THE POTENTIAL OF OKRs TO DEVELOP YOUR COMPANY

We've said that there are six common themes for organizational transformation, and that OKRs can help your organization move toward these desired benefits. Let's take a look at how OKRs can support this journey.

OKRs can provide **FOCUS** by setting specific goals and highlighting certain initiatives. They guide critical decision-making and provide a clear foundation for prioritization. Defining OKR Sets across every level of a company sets up a transparent prioritization mechanism that everyone can see—and that can continuously direct the focus of the organization.

OKRs provide **ALIGNMENT** when they unify the whole organization around the same goals. This, of course, requires strong communication, openness, and transparency. OKRs foster alignment when teams create their OKR Sets using questions like "What is our contribution toward the goals?" The OKR Cycle makes explicit the need for alignment by means of iterative communication about the vision, strategy, and progress made toward achieving the goals you've set.

VALUE-CREATION means not simply doing things, but doing the *right things.* In our context, we believe that the *right things* are those that create and deliver value. Many organizations today settle for making things and hoping that those things will deliver value. But a true orientation around value requires that we *understand the impact* of our work on our users, customers, employees, and society as a whole. The OKR Cycle allows us to make this assessment, because Key Results can express and measure the value we're seeking. Value-creation is not a one-time event, but needs to happen continuously. The OKR Cycle also allows us to do this, because it is an ongoing, iterative process.

MEANINGFUL CONTRIBUTION is the feeling that the work that you are doing both contributes to a higher goal and is aligned with your personal purpose. We believe that meaningful contribution is a key factor for motivation and happiness. People feel that they are making a Meaningful Contribution because of a number of factors, including having the ability to choose the right way to achieve their goals and feeling connected to the outcomes of their work. OKRs provide a framework to enable Meaningful Contribution, because it makes connections to the higher goals visible, and at the same time allows teams and individuals the autonomy to decide how to pursue those goals.

To keep up with today's fast-paced environment, and to cope with the complexity of our work, companies need to be flexible enough to adapt to new information and changes in conditions. To do this quickly, we need to make sure that the people with the most knowledge or competence are able to make critical decisions rapidly. This means enabling **AUTONOMOUS DECISION-MAKING**. OKRs define objectives, but they typically don't tell people *how* to achieve those objectives. This gives people the freedom to experiment with different ways to achieve the goals. At the same time, OKRs create a transparent foundation for the other decisions that the teams or individuals need to make.

Finally, OKRs are well-suited to embed **FAST LEARNING CYCLES** and drive organizational learning. Organizational learning (in our context) is the ability of an organization to apply what individuals and teams are learning, broadly across the entire organizational system in order to more effectively reach its goals. In this age of complexity, applying Fast Learning Cycles with intentional experimentation to everything you do is crucial. As Peter Senge puts it, "The only sustainable competitive advantage is an organization's ability to learn faster than the competition." The concept of OKRs is well-suited to this kind of fast learning, because it is built around a cyclical model. This model doesn't limit itself in scope to the work of a single team. Instead it is a model for learning and development that connects the work of individuals and teams to create an integrated model of work that provides iterative learning opportunities for the whole organization.

PAUSE PRACTICE

Reflection is a crucial part of the OKR Cycle and effective work in general. For this reason, we'll include small Reflection Practice sections throughout this book. Use them to take a moment to pause and reflect on the things we shared so far, where you and your company currently stand, and what your possible next steps might look like.

To start, take a minute or two to reflect back on the story from the beginning of this chapter and ask yourself these questions:

> » *Are there ongoing discussions in your company about new ways of working?*
> » *Are you or your company also working on achieving some of the benefits we've described?*
> » *What have you tried so far to achieve them?*

TAKEAWAYS FROM THIS CHAPTER

> » An organization is a complex system. To change the system and create long-term success, you need new habits, structures, and processes that enable new principles of working throughout the organizational system and for all employees.
> » Goals are a key cornerstone of the organizational system. Changing the way you work with goals has the potential to drive ongoing change across the entire system to create more focus, alignment, value creation, connection to meaning, autonomous decision-making, and faster learning cycles. That's why we see goals at the center of every organizational transformation.
> » Although goals are a key element of an organizational system, they don't exist in a vacuum. When you change the way you work with goals, it will impact the other elements, and the same is true in reverse.
> » OKRs have the potential to drive these changes in your organization, because they bridge the gap from purpose, vision, and strategy to tasks by describing the next step toward it. They allow you to create greater transparency of goals and their progress, encourage regular reflection, and create the opportunity for rapid response to changing conditions.

CHAPTER 2: OKRs FOR FOCUS, ALIGNMENT, AND LEARNING

*"They always say time **changes** things, but you actually have to **change them yourself.**"*

—Andy Warhol

Organizational transformation is a long and challenging endeavor, and it doesn't just drive itself. Organizational change needs an impetus—a motor—to drive change continuously. We believe that OKRs can be that motor.

More than just a new goal-setting system, OKRs can serve as an ongoing tool for learning and development in your organization. So how do you put that into practice?

Though there are certain guidelines that have proven to work, as with all frameworks, there is no "one way" or "right way" of using OKRs. There are many ways to shape your use of OKRs, each based on your individual starting point and what you are trying to achieve with them at a particular moment in time.

Finding your individual way of working with OKRs is critical for long-term success. In this book, we'll look at three different examples of OKRs in use at different companies. We'll consider how each company worked with OKRs, what challenges they faced, and what they were able to achieve. You'll see OKRs used for goal-setting, but you'll also see how OKRs unlock organizational learning, development, and transformation.

One note before we get started: If you're reading closely, you'll probably see some things in each example that these companies are "doing wrong." It's tempting, when creating examples, to share idealized cases. But no implementation of OKRs will ever be ideal. Instead, it will be the result of a series of trade-offs. And, as we said above, there's no single right way. So we've chosen to present the examples here as we observed them, and use that as an opportunity to discuss the trade-offs that each company chose to make.

OKRs AT INNOVIO: FOCUS, ALIGNMENT, AND LEARNING

After being introduced to the idea of OKRs at the conference, Peter returned to Innovio and shared what he had learned with some colleagues. One of them, a progressive team leader named Monica, had worked with OKRs before. She loved the idea of trying OKRs at Innovio. So together with her team, she began an experiment. The team dove in and formulated team objectives for the next quarter.

Over the next three months, they checked in regularly and shared their experiences in company meetings. Other pilots were taking place at the same time, including one in the management team. The results of the pilots were largely positive, even though the process wasn't always easy.

That's how John, one of the members of Monica's pilot team described his first experience with OKRs at Innovio to us: "After the first OKR Definition Workshop, we were a bit overwhelmed by the number of goals we wanted to achieve and how to best prioritize them. We also had a lot of questions, and we weren't sure how to gather all the necessary information to really align with the other teams. As we worked through some of these issues, it got better though. I think we now have a far better foundation for the next quarter and we learned a lot along the way."

INNOVIO'S OKR SYSTEM

Once the results of the pilots were in, the leadership team at Innovio decided to implement OKRs across the whole organization. For the first company-wide implementation, Innovio's process looked like this:

» First, the leadership team defined the overall goals by creating the Company-OKR Sets at headquarters.

» Innovio has locations spread across five different countries. So, the next step was for the country leads to create the next-level OKR Sets with their country leadership teams.

» After that, the functional teams in each country (such as IT, Product, Content, Design, and Operations) defined OKR Sets for themselves.

"It was very clear from the beginning that the management team needed to be in charge and that the process should cascade down through the hierarchy," said John about the rollout. He described the process of creating team-level OKR Sets. "We sat down with Monica, our team lead, to brainstorm ideas and link them to the goals defined by the levels above. Of course, Monica had the final say."

Monica took it from there: "I took our team's OKR Sets and aligned them with the OKR Sets of the other teams. We did that in a four-hour team lead meeting. There was a lot of discussion—some of it pretty intense—because all of our big initiatives needed to be aligned across all functions. It was exhausting, but it created a lot of clarity and new insights."

Implementing OKRs across an entire organization is a challenge because you need to find a way to link the OKR Sets of all the levels and teams, align across functions and locations, and create massive feedback loops. You also have to make decisions about who will be involved in each step and how often and at which levels you will check in and reflect.

Typically, organizations create a so-called "OKR Tree" for the whole organization in order to visualize all of the OKR Sets and to establish a foundation for the upcoming quarter. An OKR Tree is a structure that contains all of the OKR Sets and shows how they are linked to the organization's high-level goals. The company-level OKR Sets are found at the top. Below that, you'll find country or department OKR Sets and team OKR Sets. In this way, the structure of the OKR Tree will reflect the ways that the organization has chosen to align around goals—be it in cross-functional teams, departments, or a mix of both.

What we've just described is what we call an "**OKR System**." An OKR System is made up of these parts and variables—all of the different pieces that determine the way you work with OKRs: from the **OKR System Basics** (e.g., how long your cycle takes or on which levels you define OKRs) to the design of your **OKR Cycle** elements (e.g., bi-weekly OKR Check-ins in the management team) to the actual content of your **OKR Set Definition** (e.g., milestones in your Key Results).

INNOVIO'S OKR SET DEFINITION

Let's look at Innovio's OKR Set Definition in a little more detail.

Their starting point was the company vision, which says that Innovio strives to "be an innovation leader in the agency business." Their most relevant strategic goals for the next one to two years are "to achieve next-level of growth to reach market-leader position" and "to be known for the highest degree of innovation." The vision and the strategic goals served as input for the leadership workshop that Innovio held to come up with their highest-level company-wide OKR Set.

Company-OKR Sets typically reflect certain areas of focus, usually related to the company's strategy. Indeed Innovio's first OKR Set was the result of a strategic discussion. To drive that discussion, they asked questions about what strategic success would look like, including "What success stories would we want to share at the upcoming industry conference of agency leaders?" and "What key indicators would change if we could close our actual strategic weak spots?" Based on the insights these discussions created, Innovio decided to focus on just one OKR Set for its first company-wide experiment with OKRs, which was this:

Company Objective 1: We are kicking off growth

> » KR 1: Three new innovation products are live
> » KR 2: 100% sales growth compared to prior-
>   year quarter
> » KR 3: Significantly increased client reach:
>   100% follower growth for every client

Following the Company-OKR Set, the next level of Innovio's OKR Tree was country- or site-level (remember that Innovio has five locations). To create country-level OKR Sets, country leaders asked themselves this question: "What is the contribution of our site to the overall company goals for the next three months?" Here's a typical OKR Set for one of the company's locations:

Country A Objective 1: Our region gets a new growth push
  - » KR 1: One new innovation product is live (voice skill kit)
  - » KR 2: 70% sales growth compared to prior-year quarter
  - » KR 3: +100% follower growth for every Country A client

Other countries had similar, but site-specific goals. The idea is, that taken together, if all of the sites reached their goals, then the company would reach its overall goals.

This process was repeated as they moved down through the hierarchy. Each of the teams used the same question ("How can we contribute to the goals that have been set at the level above us?") to create their own OKR Sets. After setting tentative goals at their levels, teams engaged in an alignment process with their peer teams to harmonize the goals. Once that process was completed, the first OKR Sets for some of the teams that contribute to the Country-OKR Set shown above looked liked this:

	CONTENT	IT/PRODUCT	SALES/CONSULTING
TEAM OBJECTIVE	**We are riding the video growth wave**	**We create our own voice skill kit**	**We are securing growth**
KEY RESULTS	**KR 1:** » 50 video clips written per customer **KR 2:** » +50% more followers per customer through video **KR 3:** » create 3 search engine optimized (SEO) voice skill articles	**KR 1:** » features 1, 2, 3, and 4 are fully defined **KR 2:** » features 1, 2, and 3 are live **KR 3:** » 5 user tests carried out on the prototype	**KR 1:** » 70% sales growth (QOQ) **KR 2:** » at least 1 social media seminar at 10 most important clients sold out **KR 3:** » 30 customer appointments carried out

Innovio's OKR definition process is only one of many ways to create the OKR Tree in your organization. Their approach was essentially a top-down approach that incorporated some bottom-up elements. For example, leadership declared a desire to launch three new products, but the specifics of which products to launch was left up to the teams themselves.

THOUGHTS ON THE OKR SETS

Looking at the OKR Sets from Innovio's first company-wide experiment, you could say that the higher-level OKR Sets describe more of an overall impact, one that is too broad to be achieved by a single person or team. The scope is rather the sum of all activities in the company (like a certain "sales growth" to achieve market leader position). The more the process cascades down, the more specific and actionable the OKR Sets become for each team (for example the Product Team's specific output: "new feature is live").

There are different ways to cascade OKR Sets from the company-level down to every team, if that's what you want to do. Sometimes it might be possible and reasonable to distribute a Key Result between different teams mathematically. For a Key Result like "three new innovation products," you could simply assign one new product to each team. But if you focus more on the general impact in your definition of the Key Results, then it might be harder to cascade them down.

Let's look at another example. In Country A, the Country Leader set the goal to increase their client follower reach by 100%. That simply cascaded the same number—100%—from the company-wide Key Result. Further down though, the relation becomes more complex. To achieve this Key Result, the Content Team in that country chose to focus on video. For that team, they chose the ambitious Key Result: "+50% more followers per customer through video."

But the IT/Product team didn't define any specific targets around social growth. Their objective, "create our own voice skill kit" only indirectly supports the goal for follower reach. And the Sales Team defined related activities (social media seminars), that *might* impact follower reach, but again these Key Results do not directly address increasing the social media reach.

Taken together, you can see how this group of OKR Sets could ladder up to the next level result, even though the way the targets are defined is not built around precise mathematical logic.

PAUSE PRACTICE

> » *When you imagine being part of such an OKR Set*
>   *definition process and have a look at the examples*

we shared from Innovio's OKR Tree, what gets your
attention? How would you feel about those OKR
Sets and about the process as a country manager or
employee in one of the teams in this company? Would
you feel inspired? Would you feel secure that your
company is heading in the right direction?

COMPLETING THE OKR CYCLE

Once the OKR Sets are defined, the rest of the OKR Cycle begins.
At Innovio, after the OKR definition and alignment process was
completed, the management team sent a company-wide email
telling everyone what had been decided. The email included a
link to a tool that Innovio had selected to manage the OKR Tree.
Everyone in the company was able to look at the entire tree to get a
sense of what was going on. This allowed everyone in the company
to monitor progress in an ongoing way.

To further track the progress, the management team held
bi-weekly OKR Check-in meetings to look at the Key Results of the
Company- and Country-OKR Sets. Some other teams also held
regular check-in meetings. The reflection at the end of the OKR
Cycle was held only at company level at first; later the country
leads also started to do that.

OKR SYSTEM LEARNINGS: FOCUSING ON CHECK-INS

As the year progressed, Innovio realized through the OKR Check-
ins, OKR Reflections, and many discussions beyond that, that
they had to make adjustments to the way they were using OKRs—
their OKR System. Innovio ended up tweaking the OKR System
a great deal over the first four iterations based on lessons
learned along the way. They made some small but important
changes: for example, they allowed more time for the OKR
Definition workshops and they combined the previous-quarter

OKR Reflections with the Company-OKR Set Definition workshop in order to improve both meetings.

"Another big aha moment came during a review we held last year." Peter told us. "One of the teams reported only 20% achievement of their Key Results. When we looked more closely at what had happened, it became obvious that the OKR Set defined at the beginning of the OKR Cycle became completely obsolete later in the cycle, because the market had changed. The thing that made this particularly frustrating was that the team's performance had been outstanding considering the unexpected market changes. So they did an amazing job, but they felt really disappointed." This led Innovio to experiment with different techniques to **focus more on learning, not performance**, for example by not using Red-Yellow-Green in the progress overview and **presenting the results with the necessary context already in the OKR Check-in meetings.**

Indeed, the most significant changes, though, concerned the way Innovio handled the OKR Check-ins throughout the organization. They found that those meetings were especially important, because they helped the entire OKR Cycle run smoothly. The first change implemented was to combine the OKR Check-Ins with regular meetings to improve meeting participation and reduce the number of meetings at their company in general.

Innovio also began to use the following structure for OKR Check-ins across the company. This structure had proven effective in their experiments, so they rolled it out broadly:

1. **Looking back** to evaluate the current situation: Walking through a (prepared in advance) status overview of all Key Results to understand the current situation and to create a starting point for discussions.

2. **Looking forward** to estimate the end-state based on the knowledge of today: Sharing individual assessments of the Key Result progress and background information. The more the estimations among team members differ, Innovio found, the higher the need for communication and investigation.

3. **Adjusting and planning** next priorities and activities for the upcoming week(s). If completely new topics arise, an extra task planning meeting will be scheduled.

The goal of this OKR Check-In agenda was to find alignment on each agenda item. If no divergent estimates or opinions came up, Innovio found that the Check-in can be done within 15 minutes. If, on the other hand, substantial disagreements arose, there was a need for in-depth discussions and perhaps even an additional meeting.

Another lesson learned was that given the diversity of metrics in the Key Results, some important metrics related to overall company success and other factors were not being monitored closely by all teams. Inspired by the health metrics recommended by Christina Wodtke (see Reading List), Innovio started to define key organization-wide metrics relevant, such as revenue, customer satisfaction, and others. They tried to include them in the Key Results, but if that was not reasonable, they separately monitored them in the OKR Check-in meetings so as to not lose sight.

See Reading List for a useful OKR Check-in Template.

REACTIONS AT INNOVIO

When we met with Innovio a year into the process, they told us that their OKR implementation has been a success, especially when compared to their former goal-setting process. Innovio's CEO Claire described it like this: "Working with OKRs has really changed the way we think and communicate about goals in the company. I believe that making goals transparent and aligning them toward a shared objective has improved our overall performance and focus."

Tina, a member of the IT/Product team agreed: "I really liked that the introduction of clear and measurable team goals brought focus and that we in the teams felt a stronger connection to the company goal in general." Tina also felt that OKRs have made it easier to prioritize. "The projects that were always coming up out of the blue are still there, but at least the OKR Sets give us a better way to discuss their priority with our managers. This way we were able to re-prioritize at least some of them."

People also felt good about the added transparency that the OKR System brought with it. Claire shared: "Everyone always knows whether we are on the right track. That feels good. And the quarterly cadence gave us the opportunity to adapt to what we were learning more frequently. That makes sense when your markets change so quickly."

Not everything was perfect though.

"Getting the process up and running was a huge effort," Claire told us. "And the process is still not totally smooth. The alignment, for example, still takes a lot of time and isn't easy. It can be hard to handle conflicting ideas about how to achieve our goals, and we still have to manage many interdependencies. I'm not a patient person per se, so I really had to work on trusting the process and not intervening all the time."

Not everyone also felt good about the alignment, Claire added: "I've also heard some feedback that some of my country managers feel a lack of freedom now, because they need to align toward the company goals from headquarters."

Others worried about the possibility of increased micromanagement. Tina told us, "My manager is rather laid-back and trusts us, but other managers are not like that. They needed some time to make themselves comfortable being less in charge of the detailed task planning. And honestly, some leaders just micromanage their teams no matter which process we will use."

It was also not clear if Innovio's implementation of OKRs increased people's feeling of meaningful contribution. Tina's colleague Mark shared: "I read somewhere that OKRs are all about better outcomes. I still have the feeling that we are in output mode. We're looking at the number of sold seminars or appointments instead of the value that the customer gets from these things. For me personally, that's not very inspiring. It's not what I want to contribute to. And at least at the beginning, I felt really pressured by the ambitious numbers in some of the Key Results."

EVALUATING THE OKR IMPLEMENTATION

One way to evaluate an OKR implementation is to consider it in terms of our six desired benefits. Let's see how Innovio felt about the progress made in these factors:

> » **Focus:** Innovio had a clear focus on performance and growth and used OKRs to support that. The first OKR iterations gave them a major benefit here: Focus increased because of the way Innovio tied their work to their strategic goals. They prioritized growth in the Company-OKR Set and aligned the goals on all other levels to the company level. The increased transparency across the company also helped Innovio to focus, because they could clearly see and track the progress of other teams.

> » **Alignment:** Throughout the whole organization, alignment has significantly improved due to

cascading the goals and an increased communication among the teams and across hierarchies.

» **Fast Learning Cycles:** The quarterly setup created faster learning cycles compared to the former yearly cycles.

The remaining three factors show some additional opportunities for improvement:

» Continuous **Value-Creation** is an ongoing challenge. So is **Meaningful Contribution**. This was especially true for teams that were given very specific targets to hit, and very precise definitions of *how* to achieve those targets. That didn't leave those teams a lot of freedom to decide how to best achieve their overall goal.

» The same was true for **Autonomous Decision-Making,** which is still in the early stages due to the top-down approach Innovio has used so far. Here, many opportunities to better involve all employees in the goal-setting process can still be exploited.

ORGANIZATIONAL DEVELOPMENT OPPORTUNITIES

As we've said, working with OKRs can reveal opportunities for organizational development, especially if you really pay attention to the learning opportunities created by OKR Check-ins and Reflections. But sometimes, it can be hard to see (or act on) those opportunities as an insider—someone who is a part of the system. This is when it can be helpful to have an outsider's perspective. In our work with Innovio, we observed a number of areas to achieve even more benefits for them—opportunities that would require some fundamental and courageous changes to their system.

As goals are always intertwined with the whole organizational system, working with OKRs has made some challenging connections visible. Some organizational aspects have been boosters (+) whereas others turned out to be obstacles (-) on Innovio's path to fully unlocking the six desired benefits with OKRs.

OKRs AT THE CENTER AT INNOVIO

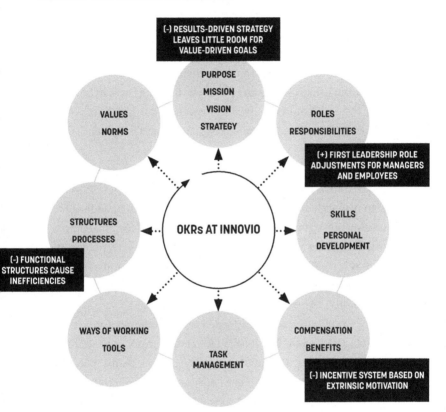

Let's have a closer look at four specific aspects of their organizational system that might have to change in order to unlock further improvement:

From results-driven to value-driven purpose and strategy: As Innovio's teams learned how to define OKRs, a number of them tried to come up with more value-driven OKR Sets. In other words, they tried to frame their OKR Sets around delivering value to customers or the business ("increase renewal rates") rather than creating a result ("create an innovative feature"). However, the overall company strategy was already framed in terms of results ("be a market leader"). To allow for a value-creation mindset at lower levels, Innovio could change the way it frames its vision, strategy, and highest-level goals, which would allow lower-level teams to use their creativity to identify and deliver value. Frameworks like the Product Field (See Reading list) can be useful here to help create a balanced strategy that addresses user needs, takes into account your unique capabilities, and make sense within your market.

Redefining roles and responsibilities: Teams and team leads discovered as they worked with OKRs that they had to rethink the responsibilities of each role. Team leads needed to provide new information to team members so that they could formulate the team goals. Team members needed to assume new responsibilities as they learned to define team goals. These new responsibilities were not universally welcomed, nor were they always easy to handle.

Similarly, new habits needed to be developed during the ongoing OKR Cycle. Leaders had fewer opportunities to simply push pet projects. They had to rely more on their teams to identify next steps. In other words, they had less room for micromanaging.

No one at Innovio had considered these changes before the implementation, and so the company provided no training or communication about these aspects of the system. It wasn't until it started to become really difficult that the company held a workshop to consider "New Leadership at Innovio." This workshop brought a lot of clarity, as well as some official adjustments to expectations for leadership roles. Considering these types of impacts from the beginning will provide you with a helpful head start.

Compensation & Benefits systems as obstacles or drivers for change: As Innovio's employees thought about creating ambitious, value-driven goals, it became clear that compensation was an issue—because compensation for some employees was tied to their performance on OKRs. This made it hard for them to really take risks, stretch themselves, and use their OKR Sets as a learning opportunity.

This is an example of a structure-culture misfit—meaning that organizational structures and processes conflict with or counteract the culture and behaviors you're trying to create. Structure-culture misfits can really hinder change initiatives. In Innovio's case, cutting the link between incentive systems and individual contributions to achieving OKRs could increase people's willingness to experiment and learn, and thus might unlock value-creation. Further exploration of other Agile HR Practices (see Reading List) might also inspire new ways of team development, administration, and recruiting that better fit the desired future state of the organization.

Rethinking functional structures: Everyone at Innovio thought that the OKR Set alignment process took too much time—in part because so much cross-department communication was required. Of course, any company-wide alignment process can feel strenuous, but for Innovio, it was probably harder than it needed to be because the alignment processes were built around functional, rather than initiative, teams. When people met only with people in their functions, they didn't have enough knowledge of the various initiatives to create effective alignment. This created conflicts and dependencies that could be resolved only by long discussions over many meetings. Addressing this underlying issue—moving to more cross-functional or initiative-based planning and organizational structures—could reduce the conflicts and dependencies and make alignment simpler in the future.

TAKEAWAYS FROM THIS CHAPTER

» Every organization is different, and every OKR implementation will have different goals. It is important to find your organization's way of working with OKRs based on your starting point and what you are trying to achieve.

» When you start using OKRs you create momentum in your organization, because transparency, participation, working cycles, and other characteristics change the ways of working and communicating about goals for everyone and will lead to challenging discussions and different (perceived) benefits for employees and managers.

» If you strive for more focus, alignment, and generally faster learning, starting to use a more top-down OKR Tree that includes a detailed company-wide alignment process can be an option. To fully attain the (other) desired benefits, more changes inside and outside the OKR System will probably be necessary.

» Reflecting on the challenges within the OKR System will lead you to organizational pain points that are worth looking into, to further develop your organization and thus also improve your OKR System. Often times, the first obvious challenges are functional structures, results-driven company vision and strategy, and contravening incentive systems.

CHAPTER 3: OKRs FOR VALUE-CREATION

Now let's consider a different company's implementation of OKRs. Where Innovio used a primarily top-down OKR approach, which helped them achieve more focus, alignment, and learning, Momenta chose a very different setup for their way of working with OKRs.

Momenta is a successful but somewhat traditional e-commerce company that has been working with OKRs for a number of years. Known as "The Party Makers," the company has a well-established business selling party supplies online. The company has about 100 employees working in cross-functional teams organized around event types: children's birthdays, carnivals, and weddings. Momenta is still owner-managed and has started to adopt agile principles.

The company has grown rapidly, doubling the number of employees in just the last year. This brought new requirements for a new level of transparency for new employees, for faster onboarding, and for new processes. The growth has changed the way Momenta uses OKRs as well. The organization has been using OKRs for three years and has adjusted their OKR System a number of times—building on lessons learned along the way and responding to changes and new requirements.

Today, Momenta's key challenges involve improving the ability to attract top tech talent and establishing better customer focus across the business.

MOMENTA'S OKR SYSTEM

When we first met with Momenta, the company's OKR System looked like this:

> » First, the management team defined annual strategic focus areas at the company level to create overall guidance.
> » Then the management team created the Company-OKR Sets for the following quarter.
> » Then, the mostly cross-functional teams defined team-level OKR Sets that showed how they would contribute to the Company-OKR Sets.

Karen, who is responsible for the OKR process at Momenta, summarized the current setup:

> *"Today we have a pretty straight-forward process with a lot of freedom for everyone involved, but also lots of feedback loops. For example, the management team can add new focus areas and update the Key Results during the alignment phase if necessary. Our teams can also give feedback during that period—if crucial topics arise, the Company-OKR Sets will be adjusted as well.*
>
> *In general though, we don't have to spend much time aligning OKR Sets among teams, because the cross-functional teams work relatively independently. The only place alignment is critical is with the technical platform team, who are responsible for the technical foundation of all the e-commerce shops. We do this through a two-hour meeting each quarter with the product owners of each team.*
>
> *We also recently established **OKR Expert** roles within the teams to support the process and help the teams define better OKR Sets."*

If you compare what Momenta is doing with how Innovio has implemented OKRs, some differences become clear immediately. Momenta used an extra layer of yearly strategic focus areas for orientation. They also chose to install a feedback loop for top-down/bottom-up alignment of the draft OKR Sets (where leadership can add new topics and teams can give general feedback.) Additionally, they created OKR Expert roles to strengthen each team's skills and responsibilities.

MOMENTA'S OKR SET DEFINITION

Momenta's mission is to "generate and celebrate magical moments." To make this happen for as many people as possible, Momenta's strategy has been to "strive for the highest quality possible" and to "try to create unique celebration moments for every customer."

In the strategic planning process, managers identified an opportunity to expand their service offerings. In addition to simply selling party supplies, Momenta could also offer a full-service party-planning business featuring planning, catering, and other services. Management made this idea one of the strategic focus areas in the company-level OKR Set and projected what success in this area might look like in three months:

Company Objective: Let's start celebrating 360 degrees

- » KR 1: 50% of customers are multi-service customers
- » KR 2: All new offers reach at least 75% on the internal Momenta-Magic-Index
- » KR 3: Total revenue growth of 30% compared to prior-year quarter (QOQ) through new services

Then, this is what the some of the teams came up with for contributing to the Company-OKR Set:

TEAM	CHILDREN'S BIRTHDAYS	WEDDINGS	OPERATIONS/HR
OBJECTIVE	Children 360 Degrees	One wedding, one provider	Enable full-service operations
KEY RESULTS	**KR 1:** » new "animation" service is designed	**KR 1:** » 50% of customers are multi-service customers	**KR 1:** » full-service-competence for all 14 relevant roles done
	KR 2: » 50% of customers are multi-service customers	**KR 2:** » 75% customer satisfaction (new services)	**KR 2:** » 50% of customers are multi-service customers
	KR 3: » 1,000 positive reviews online about new services	**KR 3:** » 100% revenue growth (QOQ) through new services	**KR 3:** » 10 new full-service partnership contracts signed

THOUGHTS ON MOMENTA'S OKR SETS

When we look at the examples from the OKR Tree at Momenta, some other differences from Innovio become obvious as well. Momenta started from a user-centered strategy (offering one-stop party services). That gave them a foundation to think about what **value** to create as a company for the next goal cycle. This also made the goals more **meaningful** to the employees, as they could now easily understand the strategic logic driving the planning process. It allowed them to connect their OKR Sets to the company purpose, to clarify task planning, and later, to participate in achieving the goal.

Looking closely at the Key Results on the team level you can see a mix of different measurement criteria. Some describe a change in user/customer behavior (such as "positive reviews" or becoming "multi-service customers") This way of formulating Key Results allows everyone to focus on value-creation. It gives employees the freedom to test different ways of creating value, instead of locking employees into inflexible task- or results-based plans.

OKR Sets are always just a hypothesis—your best guess about a desired future. But when you express your Key Results as value measures, you give your team the ability to test that hypothesis. When your Key Results are more task based, you are no longer guessing—you're declaring that that task is necessary. This is risky, especially when the Key Result is something big. What if that is more work than you think? What if it doesn't work? For this reason, defining OKR Sets that are based on value—**that describe and measure the outcome or impact of your work instead of the output of your work**—can mitigate this risk and lead to better results.

At the same time, goals like this can be difficult to work with, because in some cases, no direct, early measurements are possible. Therefore, other Key Results in the Momenta Tree consist of milestone-like activities. These activities need to be accomplished before any change in user/customer can be measured. (The Children's Birthday's team wrote one Key Result like this: their new service animation would need to be "designed.")

If you reflect on the Momenta OKR Sets, you might ask yourself whether they are truly inspiring. Maybe you find them too numbers-driven or not clear enough. What is inspirational and ambitious for one group of people might not be a good fit for another group of people—even in the same industry. This is one reason you should always define your individual OKR Sets from scratch instead of using external examples as a starting point. Defining what is inspiring and relevant *for your organization* makes the difference, not using some other company's benchmarks.

PAUSE PRACTICE

> » *How would you or your team react if they were*
> *working with OKR Sets that provide only a*
> *rough description of where to go, but contain*
> *no specific predefined tasks, features to create,*
> *or milestones describing how to get there? Does*
> *it make you excited? Or anxious? If so, why do*
> *you think that is?*

OKR SYSTEM LEARNINGS: FOCUSING ON VALUE-DRIVEN OKR SETS

Even though Momenta had been using OKRs for quite some time, every new iteration brought new learnings about the OKR System and the organization itself. Recently, Momenta has learned a lot about the best ways to define value-based OKR Sets. There are many challenges to doing this well, including getting all the right people involved, finding time for discussion and reaching conclusions, and then formulating good clear OKRs. Momenta discovered that a good process relies on effective interpersonal communication.

At Momenta, a designated workshop serves as a platform to do that. Workshop formats make it easier to manage the definition process and also provide many opportunities to actively divide between the idea creation phase, evaluation, and adjustment. Additionally, a collaborative workshop tends to create more context and better shared understanding from the beginning of the process, helping leaders align on strategy, goals, and measurement options, as well as timeline and resource estimates.

To ensure success, Momenta developed the following techniques to define OKR Sets in their workshops. These are good methods to keep in mind when writing your own OKRs:

» **Ask** *why* **as often as necessary to get to the point, working backward from tasks to actual goals.**
For example, you might start with a task like "Introduce a new booking software." You would then ask, "*Why* should we introduce this software?" You can use the Five Why question method to find a broad range of reasons behind a single idea for a task. Ask *why* until you move from generic answers to specific goals. In other words, don't settle for answers like, "get more efficient," but keep pushing until you find a better answer, like "make people happier with easier ordering." Important here: Open the space for *all* ideas at the beginning of the workshop no matter how big or small and use them as valuable input to work your way toward the goals.

» **Improve value-creation with measurable Key Results.** Key Results can be relative numbers like 10%, absolute numbers like 20,000, binary results, or one of a series of milestones. To improve value-creation, Momenta tries to avoid milestones and instead aims for as many actually measurable Key Results as possible. This allows the organization to discuss progress relative to customer behavior or value-creation instead of simply checking off tasks. One good source of relevant Key Results can be key activities of the customer journey or impact maps.

For a more comprehensive guide to effective OKR Definition Workshops, see the Reading List at the end of this book.

REACTIONS AT MOMENTA

When we spoke to management and employees at Momenta about the OKR System and its implementation, we heard a lot of positive feedback.

"Our OKR journey has been a roller-coaster ride," says Maggie, who is part of the management team and joined the company shortly after it started to work with OKRs. "Even though we had a solid foundation—an open culture and cross-functional teams—it took a while for us to really unlock the potential of OKRs."

Jennifer, who has been working for the Children's Birthday team for three years now told us: "We've really improved over the few last cycles in terms of how we define OKR Sets and track progress. We've been able to find a way to focus on what's important and align better among the teams, without predefining the work too much in the OKR Sets. It makes it easier to focus on delivering what our customers need and want. I also found the OKR Experts helpful when we got stuck somewhere. I think that improved our ability to learn within each OKR Cycle as well. Learning is important because there's always room for improvement."

The teams at Momenta quickly realized that setting up their OKR System is only one part of the process. The other (and perhaps more challenging) part is actually putting the OKR System into practice every single day during the OKR Cycle, and doing it in a way that supports your learning and development.

And, as if that isn't hard enough, the OKR System itself also needs ongoing development and sometimes radically changes over time: Every element in the OKR System and surrounding factors (like OKR Experts or strategy connections) can be designed differently to support the various benefits you want to achieve. In other words, as your company changes, your OKR System will need to adapt in response to reflect the changes.

James, who recently joined from a smaller start-up pointed out: "It's great that we can come up with our own solution as to how to achieve the goals. However, we don't have any say about purpose or strategy, which I really liked having at my last employer—it gives you a lot of freedom to react to market changes and customize what you are doing for each customer. I also think the OKR Expert role could do more. Right now, they help formulate OKR Sets and run the retrospectives. I think they could also build a community of practice to share all the lessons and by that create even more momentum for improvement throughout the company."

EVALUATING THE OKR IMPLEMENTATION

Looking back at what Momenta has achieved since implementing OKRs, we can see a lot of success. Still, some general challenges remain. When we asked people at the company to rate themselves on the six desired benefits, here's what we heard:

>> **Focus:** Momenta has heavily improved focus, due to transparent goals and a clear north star.
>> **Alignment:** The cross-functional teams with few interdependencies and a simple process brings efficient alignment without much additional coordination processes across the organization.
>> **Value-Creation:** Compared to Innovio, Momenta was less results-focused and derived its OKR Sets from a value-driven strategy. Also, value-based OKR Sets ensured value-creation on the lower levels.
>> **Meaningful Contribution:** Benefitting from that and the high level of freedom, people rated the company well for meaningful contribution, scoring that medium to high as well.

» **Autonomous Decision-Making:** The teams have a high degree of autonomous decision-making to set goals and define the tasks necessary to achieve them, but some wish for even more.

» **Fast Learning Cycles:** Learning is a big part of Momenta's OKR System (and the organization's culture). The integration of top-down and bottom-up feedback loops, the extensive use of OKR Check-ins and Reflections, and the contribution of OKR Experts allow fast and valuable learning cycles. Of course, there is still room for improvement.

ORGANIZATIONAL DEVELOPMENT OPPORTUNITIES

As with Innovio, goals at Momenta do not exist in a vacuum. Instead, they are tightly connected with the whole organizational system. When Momenta began changing its processes from working with traditional goals to OKRs, many issues became obvious that affected the development of the organization toward the six desired benefits.

Some of the positives (+) for Momenta include value-creation, which has been supported by a **value-based strategy** that got better year by year. They've really leaned in to the **cross-functional team structures** that allowed them to holistically focus on product users. The company counted **learning as part of its values**, and indeed, learning has been strengthened through the focus on reflecting regularly, placing failures into context during Check-Ins, and acting fast on new solution ideas by adapting release plans regularly. None of this was automatic—indeed, all of this needed time to become a habit for everyone.

At the same time, using OKRs has also revealed opportunities for improvement (-) that Momenta has yet to be able to address.

OKRs AT THE CENTER AT MOMENTA

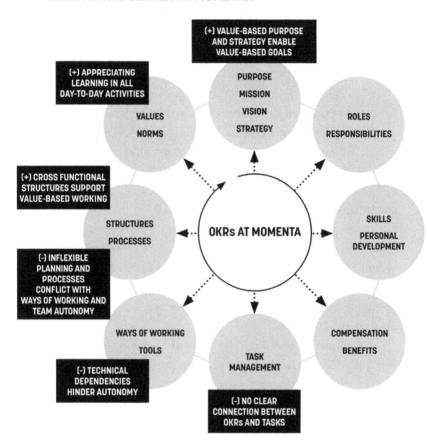

Let's have a closer look at three specific aspects of Momenta's organizational system that might have to change in order to unlock further improvement:

Connecting OKRs and task planning and execution processes:
Since Momenta's value-driven OKR Sets do not contain concrete tasks and resource allocations, those details need to be worked

out by the teams. To plan their work efficiently and manage the execution, the people at Momenta still need to connect the OKR Sets and the OKR Cycle process with their project management systems and processes. This was true whether the teams worked with Scrum, Kanban, or traditional project management approaches—even simple to-do lists.

One option would be to integrate OKRs into task meetings, for example by starting every task meeting with an OKR Check-In to clarify progress and to align to-do items with the OKR Set the task will be contributing to. This way, teams are able to see the connection between even the smallest activities or user stories and the OKR Sets they service.

Another task-management problem Momenta encountered is related to the move to value-based planning. Sometimes it takes a while between delivering a solution and seeing results. It can be hard to plan new work if you're still waiting to see the results of your previous efforts. The most common remedy for this problem is to slice work down into the smallest piece possible. That allows for fast measurement but also delivers enough value to see a change in behavior. This practice is difficult—something of an art, really—and requires teams to develop new skills that support this way of working.

Eliminate technical dependencies: Even though Momenta's team structure allowed cross-functional teams to work with one specific user group, the technical infrastructure had limitations that made it harder to organize technical resources in completely customer-centric ways.

To address challenges like this, you often need to make fundamental changes to your technical infrastructure, making it as modular and autonomous as possible. This is normally something that can't be changed over one OKR Cycle. It is a multi-cycle endeavor that takes lots of resources and needs to be made visible in a roadmap.

While that work is in progress though, the technical dependencies still require a regular alignment effort among teams. This can take place after OKR Definition, perhaps in quarterly and monthly roadmap-adjustment meetings attended by product owners. The results of this alignment work can then be taken into each team's planning meetings.

Further adapt budget and resource planning: An often overlooked challenge for OKR implementations are traditional budget and resource planning processes, which are often in the hands of the management and leadership teams only.

At Momenta, budget and resource planning happened annually in the last quarter of the year, when leadership created plans for the coming year. But the quarterly OKR Reflections and OKR Set Definition process both created the opportunity for new planning and budget requirements to surface.

This put teams in a difficult position. They were being asked to be responsible for the optimal and ambitious goal planning and at the same time were not given control over budget and resource planning. This added inefficiencies to the processes, created insecurities for team members, and hindered their ability to feel fully responsible. A more distributed and fluid process, or concepts like Beyond Budgeting (see Reading List), would be way more helpful.

TAKEAWAYS FROM THIS CHAPTER

» Setting up your OKR System is only one part of the process. The other (and sometimes even more challenging) part is bringing those aspects to life every day during each OKR Cycle and applying the learnings you gather over time.

» Aligning OKRs with task planning and execution processes is just as important. You can, for example, start by integrating the OKR perspective into task management meetings.

» If you want to strengthen value-creation and meaningful contribution, make sure to integrate many participatory elements in your OKR Cycle process, strengthen autonomous decision-making for team goal-setting and task planning, and define OKR Sets that describe a measurable value/human behavior change.

» To truly be value-based and encourage meaningful contribution in your whole organization, you also need a value-based starting point: a purpose and strategy that people can use as their north star. You also need an organizational environment that supports this: for example cross-functional structures, theme-based roadmaps, or flexible budgeting.

CHAPTER 4: OKRs FOR HOLISTIC AUTONOMY

"Impediments are not in your way. They are your way."
—Jonathan Smart

Two years after our last visit to Momenta, we went to visit them again to check on their progress.

"The last year has been crazy," Tom from recruiting told us. "We're doing great, and we can't hire fast enough to fill all of our open positions. We've built a great open culture, and we're inspired to keep improving. At the same time, our business changes so fast that we need to be even more flexible and rethink our strategies and business models."

Momenta's success had led to some of the problems that you might expect. Growth had put pressure on hiring: finding new employees with the right attitude and skills was really difficult. At the same time, Momenta wanted to continue growing, which meant that the organization needed to find new business models and new strategic thinking capabilities—and to build those out across the company.

MOMENTA'S NEW OKR SYSTEM

To be able to keep up with the fast-paced market and changing customer needs, Momenta decided to experiment with different ways to create more autonomous teams. This of course also had implications on how they worked with OKRs.

One way they changed their OKR System was to give up completely on overall Company-OKR Sets. Instead, their current OKR System looked like this:

> » First, each team set their purpose and strategy based on the company purpose.
> » Then, each team defined their own quarterly OKR Sets.
> » The management then just provides feedback on the team OKR Sets to connect them to a bigger picture and the final decisions are made together.

"Our teams try to do all the workshops together to make everything more transparent and participatory," Tom told us.

"The final decision about whether an initiative will be part of the next OKR Cycle is made by teams and management together through consent decision-making. This allows us to iterate until the best possible solutions are found. This process allows teams and management to create shared understanding and shared ownership of the goal-setting and work planning process."

This approach eliminates most of the need for further alignment work. When a cross-team initiative is identified, OKR representatives of the various teams hold a workshop together to decide on basic requirements and goals.

MOMENTA'S REDEFINED OKR SETS

When we looked at an example from Momenta's current OKR Tree, the changes became quite obvious:

Their company's purpose hadn't changed. It was still: to "generate and celebrate magical moments." That said, when we looked at the different teams—Children's Birthdays, Weddings, and others— we could see teams doing similar jobs but navigating different submarkets. As a result, each of these teams defined their own specific team purpose and strategy. The teams created up to three OKR Sets, and tried to cover 70 to 90% of their activities in these OKR Sets. Here's an example of some team OKR Sets that showed the different strategic approaches taken by the different teams:

TEAM OBJECTIVE / KEY RESULTS	CHILDREN'S BIRTHDAYS	WEDDINGS	OPERATIONS/HR
Objective	Expand partnerships	Improve our product and services maturity perception	More fun and magic at work
Key Results	**KR 1:** » $50,000 sales funnel through partner opportunities **KR 2:** » at least 1 new partnership for each of the 25 sales regions closed **KR 3:** » product training, marketing material exchange, and press release with new partners done	**KR 1:** » full-service customers satisfaction rate > 90% **KR 2:** » no celebrity wedding pitch lost because it's "not premium enough" **KR 3:** » 100% of customer feedback/ interviewees associate services with terms "highest quality," "trustworthy," and "capable"	**KR 1:** » 90% employee satisfaction in relevant employee survey section **KR 2:** » fun-competence/ fit checkup for each employee carried ou

THOUGHTS ON THE REDEFINED OKR SETS

When you look at the details in this example, you can see a mix of value-driven ("no celebrity wedding lost...") and rather results-focused targets ("product training material...done"). The results-focused Key Results have been used for initiatives for which either no other measurement criteria existed (like the fun-competence-fit checkups) or for topics where solutions to the problem already have been discovered in an upstream process and the results-focused perspective is appropriately mixed in alongside other value-focused Key Results.

The Operations/HR team uses "employee satisfaction" as a criteria. You might wonder if they can really actively influence this Key Result, but it certainly gives them orientation on where they are heading and if a course correction might be needed. As long as all of these goals are really ambitious, inspiring, and result in valuable insights for the teams themselves they are right for them in this specific moment in time.

OKR SYSTEM LEARNINGS: EXPERIMENTING WITH AUTONOMY AND ADAPTING THE OKR REFLECTIONS

After using OKRs for more than five years, Momenta had a lot of experience adapting their OKR System based on the insights they gathered along the way. During the last iterations, the organization made many changes in particular to the OKR Reflections to better fit their needs.

Initially, their OKR Reflections were mostly focused on the company level. As the teams moved to working more independently, the OKR Reflections moved entirely to the team level and became more frequent—they added a mid-cycle OKR Reflection in order to catch issues sooner. To capture company-wide learnings, the OKR Experts from each team collected their learnings and then presented the relevant insights at a company-wide all-hands meetings.

To create even more common ground, the OKR Experts developed a shared format for the OKR Reflections that all teams could use.

1. OKR "Review": Reflect on the final results.
   » Which OKR Sets did we achieve (for Momenta achievement means 80 to 100%)? Why? Did we

estimate too cautiously and unambitiously? Did we do something new to reach the ambitious OKR Sets?

» Which OKR Sets were not met (for Momenta this means less than 80%)? Why? Was the goal too ambitious? Did something unexpected happen in the market or in the team?

Each team reflected on these questions, either as a team, or with employees from other departments, customers, or other stakeholders. After the analysis, they captured the most important aha moments (positive and negative) and categorized them into market-specific, team-specific, OKR System–specific, or organization-specific lists. This helped them attribute success stories and obstacle to the right places.

2. OKR Retrospective: Reflect on the collaboration throughout the cycle

» How did we work together? What helped us throughout the process? What held us back? Is there anything we should do differently in the next OKR Cycle?

This meeting used typical retrospective formats familiar to Agile practitioners, adjusted to fit OKR needs.

Over the last two iterations, the teams at Momenta had also used the OKR Retrospective to specifically reflect on broader connections and issues relating to organizational development. They've considered the benefits that the company wants to achieve by using OKRs (i.e., value-creation, autonomous decision-making, etc.) and they've used the "OKRs at the center" model as a starting point for broader reflections.

When teams identified issues during the retrospective, they voted for the ones they wanted to try to work on, and assigned an owner to the issues, based on the following categories:

» To be resolved by the team/to focus on a certain team topic

» To be resolved by the OKR Experts/to adjust the OKR System

» To be resolved by people with broader organizational perspective and authority/to remove organizational impediments related to strategy, values, roles, structures, processes, and so on.

REACTIONS AT MOMENTA

Jennifer from the Children's Birthday team told us: "At first I was skeptical about setting our own team purpose and product strategy. It was really hard, but we worked through it, and it was great to see what we came up with and how much closer it is now to what we are trying to achieve every day for our customers."

She continued: "This also led to big changes in the way we worked with OKRs. We had been used to setting our *tasks* by ourselves during the process. But when we moved from a top-down process to a more autonomous, team-led process, we needed to think about what we wanted to keep and what elements of the OKR System needed complete reshaping."

"Setting our own purpose and strategy is a lot of responsibility," Jennifer told us, "and some team members did not feel comfortable with that at first. It was important to allow people to grow into this new role. That took some time and required a lot of communication. But it has been worth it in my opinion, because now our team really feels like we have a lot of authority to make decisions and a lot of responsibility for the results."

"It has been an interesting learning experience." That's how Maggie, Momenta's CEO, describes their most recent OKR iterations. "Some colleagues in the management team were really hesitant about the experiment with each team setting its own purpose. It was scary to give up the security and control that came with defining a direction top-down. It was uncomfortable. But the drive of our employees for setting their goals and the feedback we got from customers clearly showed us that the decision was right. Now we just need to get the details right and continue to improve. I wonder how much longer the teams will actually need us as part of the process at all!"

PAUSE PRACTICE

> » *What comes to mind first when you think of autonomy? Do you think more about freedom to choose your own tasks? Or perhaps about giving the team more autonomy regarding strategy, budget, roles, and so on? How would you feel being part of a company as described above?*

EVALUATING THE OKR IMPLEMENTATION

Let's consider how the changes that Momenta made in their use of OKRs helped them improve across the six desired benefits we've been talking about throughout the book.

> » **Focus:** Momenta already had a high degree of focus and, for example by limiting each team to three OKR Sets, continued to maintain it. (Of course you could argue that the overall focus in the company is now lower due to autonomous strategies.)
>
> » **Alignment:** The new setup required even less work to achieve alignment. Due to new meeting formats and

the transparency among the teams, most employees perceived alignment as high.

» **Value-Creation:** Being able to define team purpose and OKR Sets around the individual customers of each team helped teams create more value-driven OKR Sets and the customer feedback confirmed the experienced increase in value-creation.

» **Meaningful Contribution/Autonomous Decision-Making:** Given teams' new responsibility for setting purpose, strategy, goals, and tasks themselves, they felt that both meaningful contribution and autonomous decision-making had increased.

» **Faster Learning Cycles:** With the implementation of the new OKR Reflection formats and mid-cycle Reviews, employees confirmed that they had created even faster learning cycles.

ORGANIZATIONAL DEVELOPMENT OPPORTUNITIES

One thing that's important to point out here: In order for a bottom-up approach to OKRs to work, Momenta needed to do more than simply install a new OKR System. They needed to work on many other parts of their organizational system in order to create the kind of autonomous, value-driven system that they ultimately implemented.

Some of these key areas that supported this system (+) are noted in the diagram. Still, Momenta (like all organizations) has room for further development (-).

OKRs AT THE CENTER AT MOMENTA

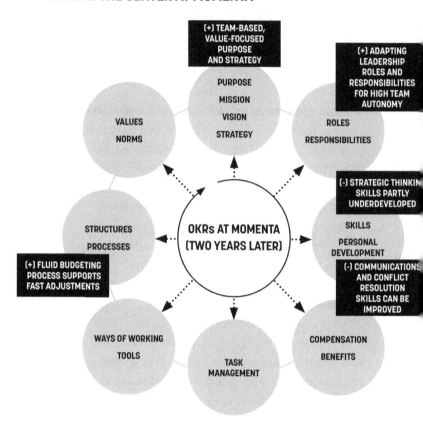

Even in a progressive company where autonomous decision-making is valued and fairly well-developed, it can be tough for leaders to let go of control. The team purpose and strategy definition was a huge shift, which brought many benefits. To achieve this, it was important to get Momenta's current managers on board, by discussing new roles and responsibilities for leadership and making sure that managers understood how their contributions remained critical.

It helped that Momenta had already been through a challenging transition when they adapted their budgeting process a year earlier. Inspired by the Beyond Budgeting framework, they installed a more fluid budgeting process that allowed teams to have easier access to resources and for more flexibility to adjust forecasts and resource allocation based on current conditions. This experience gave people at all levels in the company the confidence to go through another transition.

Let's have a closer look at specific aspects of Momenta's organizational system that might have to change in order to unlock further improvement:

Strengthening strategic skills and responsibility in the teams: As teams become responsible for setting their strategy, purpose, goals, and tasks, it stands to reason that they are dependent on strategic thinking skills, and will require training and experience with strategy processes. Though not every employee needs to become a strategist, teams need these skills and a way to participate in shaping strategy in order to have valuable discussions.

Even when strategic skills are in place, some employees can still struggle, because this can feel like a new type of responsibility. Developing personal responsibility as a skill should be on the agenda for every transformation toward more autonomy. (See Reading List.)

Developing communication and conflict-resolution skills: The potential for conflict within teams at rapidly-changing organizations is really high. Constructive conflict resolution is an important skill that needs to be taught, learned, and practiced. Especially, when even more responsibility is given to teams, the need to solve conflicts that arrive within the groups increases.

One of the biggest sources of conflict is communication. During the OKR Cycle and beyond that, teams at Momenta invested a lot of time in (hopefully) effective communication, but many said that they see room for improvement. The good news: valuable, appreciative communication can be taught and developed as well. People can learn to adopt important attitudes, like appreciating every person and every idea. People can learn how to distinguish interpretations from observations, and emotions from needs. Training employees on approaches like the nonviolent communication model by Marshall B. Rosenberg (see Reading List) can support this development.

TAKEAWAYS FROM THIS CHAPTER

» Even in a progressive company, letting go of established patterns and the security and comfort associated with them is still difficult. People need time and sufficient reflection to gain a new and shared understanding of new roles and responsibilities.

» If you want to embrace autonomous decision-making and drive even higher connection to meaning and value-creation, it's worth considering a bottom-up OKR Definition process—one that is for example driven by a (mostly) autonomous team purpose and strategy definition.

» To really embed these principles within your OKR System and beyond, you also need high autonomy in team/product strategy, technical infrastructure, budgeting, HR processes, and so on.

» At the same time, relevant skills to empower teams to pursue their goals is key. Strategic thinking, personal responsibility, efficient communication, and conflict resolution need to be taught and practiced.

CHAPTER 5: CREATING THE ORGANIZATION YOU WANT

When you listen to people talking about their companies' experience with OKRs, you typically hear many of the same themes. This applies to both the reasons that companies adopt OKRs and the challenges they meet along the way.

In the previous chapters, we looked at three different OKR implementations, one at Innovio and two different stages of implementation at Momenta. We chose those examples because they each represent one variation of the three most common patterns that we've observed over the years.

In many cases, companies start using OKRs because they struggle with rapid market changes and believe that the traditional ways to setting goals isn't working anymore. Like Innovio, these companies are looking to achieve stronger focus, better alignment, and faster learning. This is what we call the **PERFORMANCE** stage. Companies at this stage get benefits from OKRs, but often find those benefits are limited because their current structures and culture are constraints. In other words, these companies will need to make additional changes to other elements of their organizational system in order to reap additional benefits from OKRs.

After experimenting for some time—or starting from a more participatory and flexible company culture—many companies shift their focus more toward OKRs for value-creation, participation, autonomy, and meaningful contribution. Momenta (in Chapter 3) is a typical example of this stage, which we call the **OUTCOME** stage.

Finally, some companies radically change their approach—as we saw Momenta do in Chapter 4. Often building on an open and participatory company culture, this stage is characterized by even greater levels of meaningful contribution and autonomy. We call this the **AUTONOMY** stage.

SUMMARY OF POTENTIAL BENEFITS ACHIEVED WITH OKRs

BENEFITS PER STAGE	PERFORMANCE (INNOVIO)	OUTCOME (MOMENTA)	AUTONOMY (MOMENTA, LATER)
FOCUS	high	high	high
ALIGNMENT	high	high	high*
VALUE-CREATION	low	high	high
MEANINGFUL CONTRIBUTION	low	medium	high
AUTONOMOUS DECISION-MAKING	low	medium	high
FAST LEARNING CYCLES	medium	high	high

*where desired after changing the structure

The stages described above can be seen as individual points on a continuum. It's important to understand, however, that this isn't a perfect linear model. There are endless variations for every stage and not all companies move along in the same way. Some stay further to the left side, some start far off to the right. This can be for many reasons, from culture to the choices each company makes when implementing OKRs to the values held by the company.

Still, we think that this is a useful way to think about OKRs because the concept of OKRs offers many kinds of benefits. At any given moment, no organization will realize all the benefits, so it's

helpful to understand your organization and its aspirations. In that
sense, the stages can also be viewed as potential **opportunities for
development**.

PAUSE PRACTICE

> » *As you read through the examples of Innovio and
> Momenta, could you recognize your organization
> or some of the challenges and desired benefits? If
> so, which ones and what could you learn from their
> experiences that would apply to your situation?*

DESIGN YOUR OKR SYSTEM TO CREATE THE ORGANIZATION YOU WANT

In this book, we've shared stories of three different
OKR implementations—each delivering different benefits. But
now, let's think about it the other way around.

**We believe that you can create the organization you want only
if you know what that looks like for you.** For this reason, starting
with the "why" is, in our opinion, a crucial first step.

Think about Peter, the HR leader at Innovio. He was looking
for new ways of working that would help the company compete.
Although Innovio didn't spend a lot of time thinking specifically
about the benefits that OKRs could bring to the company, they
ended up implementing an OKR System that brought more focus,
better alignment, and faster learning and implementation. In
the long run, Innovio might also strive for more autonomy and
meaning, but given where the organization is today in terms of
leadership, collaboration, and other factors, that kind of change is
probably a longer-term goal.

Momenta, on the other hand, wanted more value-creation
and autonomous decision-making. These are very different desired
benefits. That, along with Momenta's very different starting point

in terms of culture, structure, and leadership, resulted in an OKR implementation that looked completely different from Innovio's.

DEFINE YOUR DESIRED OKR BENEFITS

If you are looking for the "right" way to use OKRs at your organization—whether you're just starting out or trying to improve your current OKR System—start by finding your "why." Ask yourself, your leadership team, and your colleagues questions like these:

» What does the organization we want look like?
  What are the common themes?
» Why do we want to work with OKRs?
» What do we want to achieve with OKRs?

Consider the six benefits that we've discussed: focus, alignment, fast learning cycles, value-creation, meaningful contribution, and autonomous decision-making. Throughout the book, we've used these benefits as a foundation. However, it is perfectly fine if you come up with different or more specific targets. You might want to "become one big team" or "achieve 100% strategy alignment." The important part is that you and the people in your company can relate to the benefits that you're seeking and can use them target to create and use your OKR System.

After identifying your desired OKR benefits, your next step is to think about where your organization is today and where you want it to go. Rate yourself in terms of the desired benefits. How good are you today? That's your **starting point.** Then, consider how good you'd like to be in 5 to 10 years. That's **your long-term goal.**

Next, you're going to set your first improvement target, so you'll have to break your target down further and be realistic: **For the first test phase, what do you want to achieve with OKRs?** Prioritize the answers according to your most pressing challenges.

Consider, too, what is realistic given your current organizational system—your leadership, structures and processes, compensation and benefits, etc.

DESIGN YOUR OKR SYSTEM

Once you've established your direction, it's time to think about the OKR System you need in order to achieve those benefits. Innovio, for example, was looking to increase focus toward one strategic theme for everybody in the company. That helps explain why the organization chose to cascade goals from top to bottom. Their hierarchical culture was another factor that explains why they mostly involved leadership and management in decision-making.

Innovio's desire for focus can also explain why the OKR Sets included so many results and pre-planned tasks. This helps achieve the focus the organization is looking for, even at the cost of increasing value-creation. Still, this is a huge step forward for a traditional organization. It's something that shouldn't be taken for granted or trivialized—it should be celebrated and valued.

Starting with a system that achieves real benefits like Innovio did is important, partly because it makes it possible to achieve those benefits, but also because it leads to a win that everyone can see and creates an important foundation to continue your organization's learning and development journey.

When designing your own OKR System, you have many options for each element to be designed, and as we've just described, your choices should be guided by the benefits that you've targeted.

Some of the **OKR System Basics** include:

» Rhythm: 2 months, 4 months, quarter, or other
OKR Cycle rhythm

» OKR coverage: Are OKRs used only for strategic topics and therefore cover only 10 to 20% of the team's total workload, or do you aim to describe more work with OKRs, and set perhaps 80 to 100% coverage?

» OKR levels: On how many levels do you want to use OKRs? Will you use them from the company level all the way down to personal level or in a more limited way?

In addition, you can design the **OKR Cycle Process** according to your desired benefits and starting point:

» OKR Definition: What format do you want to use? Who is involved in the process? Who makes decisions?

» OKR Check-ins: Are these done only passively by checking the results in an OKR tool, or more actively, perhaps by meeting regularly and discussing context, impediments, and next steps?

» OKR Reflections: On which level do you set up review and/or retrospective meetings? What are the main points you want to discuss in these meetings?

And last, but not least the **OKR Set Definition** itself:

» What do you define and when (yearly strategic goals, yearly OKR Sets as a starting point for the cycle OKR Sets, or none of those)?

» What characteristics should Key Results have in order to support achieving your desired benefits? Is it okay to include milestones and tasks or do you aim for behavior change as measurement criteria only?

For a more complete list of OKR System variables and techniques to facilitate this process, see the Reading List.

As you start to plan your OKR System, and think about developing your implementation over time, it's important to remember that you're going to learn as you go. As with OKR Sets themselves, your first OKR System design should be considered simply a hypothesis. It's based on the information you have at hand, and your best judgment. You're unlikely to get it entirely right the first time, so start experimenting to test your hypothesis as soon as possible.

PAUSE PRACTICE

> » *Do you already know what the organization you want looks like? And do you know what you want to achieve with OKRs? If not, what can you do to find out? How will you use this vision as a guideline for designing and developing your OKR System?*

DRIVE ONGOING CHANGE TO CREATE THE ORGANIZATION YOU WANT

After your initial setup and the first pilot phase, working with OKRs should start to deliver some of your desired benefits. If so, great. To actually create the organization that you want, though, this is not enough. Instead, here are some things to keep in mind as you continue to use OKRs.

Do things differently–starting now! Your culture and way of collaborating will not evolve overnight, nor will it change by itself. You will make progress only if you are willing to change how you do things. And now is the best time to start. If you want to achieve more participation or engagement, then ask your colleagues or employees for feedback from the very beginning. If you want to achieve faster learning, don't wait for the perfect rollout plan:

implement something with a short timetable and the expectation that you'll learn as you go. If you've started to work with OKRs and doing so is not supporting your desired journey, ask yourself what you can do to change that in a way that supports the benefits you want.

People in leadership positions play an especially important role in the ongoing change process. Often times, they alone hold the power to change the structures and processes that are holding back the organization. Plus, they are important role models in everyday execution. Work with them to help them lead the change. At the same time: Cut them some slack, they are human just like you and may have a hard time adjusting to new ways of working.

Search for your individual way. What works for one company will not work the same way in another company. That's why copying whole organizational models or approaches, like the so-called "Spotify Model," is a flawed approach. It's not just because of different cultural and systemic needs and challenges. It's also because copying and pasting omits some critical components. It omits the learning journey that leads the company toward its specific results. It omits the experience of the change that all the employees went through. It omits the experiments they ran and failed—the aha moments that these experiments triggered.

You cannot copy these things into your organization, because you cannot just skip the learning process and achieve the same results. Since OKRs affect the entire company—the whole organizational system—you need to tailor your approach to your specific needs at your starting point and create ongoing change and momentum from there. You need to understand your organization with its special opportunities and challenges.

Continuously reflect and adapt and never stop learning. We've written that the best way to learn which type of OKR System will work for your company is to experiment. If iterative ways of working are not well established at your company, it's important to agree on a time frame for your experiments. And it will be especially important to make the most of the OKR Reflections—don't skip them! Even better, integrate the OKR Reflection into the company's other reflection formats. This way everybody can remember what you're trying to achieve with OKRs and will be able to see and discuss the progress you've made toward creating the organization you want.

Each cycle will bring new insights about the OKR System and about the supporting or hindering elements of your organizational system. Continue to act on what you're learning in your experiments and your OKR Reflections. As you're doing so, resist the urge to blame the concept if it doesn't feel like a fit for the company. Consider instead how the company—and its organizational system—might need to change to reap the desired benefits.

PAUSE PRACTICE

» *What can you start doing differently with OKRs today to support an ongoing journey toward becoming the organization you want?*

» *How well do you know your organization—its unique opportunities and challenges? How can you learn more about what **your** organization needs?*

» *Do you take (enough) time to reflect on your experiments and what needs to change to develop your organization further? How could you allow more time for reflection and be more open for new learnings?*

TAKEAWAYS FROM THIS CHAPTER

» Typical stages for OKR usage are "PERFORMANCE," "OUTCOME," and "AUTONOMY." Each of the three cases shown in the book represents one variation of those stages. In each of the stages, companies can achieve different benefits by using OKRs. The stages can be seen as development opportunities for your OKR usage.

» However, there is no one way or right way to work with OKRs. There is only your organization's individual way with different benefits, setups, and learning steps.

» To create the organization you want, you first of need to know what that organization looks like. Define that, then you can define what benefits you want from using OKRs. From there, use the benefits that you're seeking to guide the design of your OKR System.

» To drive ongoing change toward the organization you want, you will actually need to do things differently, especially if you are in a leadership role. Start now!

» You cannot just skip the learning process and achieve the same results. You need to understand your organization's special opportunities and challenges in order to tailor your OKR approach.

» To gain insights into what works and what doesn't, you need to intentionally experiment and continuously reflect and adapt. "Never stop learning" can be your motto!

CONCLUSION

OKRs provide the opportunity to change the way you set, monitor, reflect, and adjust what you want to achieve in your organization in a transparent, measurable, participatory way.

Goals live at the center of everything you do, so they **affect everything and everybody in your organization**. This means that changing the way you work with goals can be a catalyst to changing the way you work together in your organization.

In this book, we wanted to open your mind and heart toward thinking about OKRs as a system that can and should be designed (starting with what you want to achieve for your organization) and continuing to use it as a driver for **ongoing change.** We hope that you'll be able to use OKRs to actively **shape the organization you want**—whatever this might look like for you today or tomorrow.

READING LIST

References

Doerr, John. *Measure What Matters: OKRs: The Simple Idea that Drives 10x Growth* (2017)

Wodtke, Christina. *Radical Focus: Achieving Your Most Important Goals With Objectives and Key Results* (2016)

Designing Your OKR System

Throughout the book, we referred to useful templates to support you on your OKR journey:

> » *OKR System Design Template*
> » *OKR Definition Workshop Template*
> » *OKR Check-in Template*

You can download these templates and more directly from our website (okrs-at-the-center.com). There you will also find articles, resources, and more about techniques on how to facilitate this process.

Further Readings

Avery, Christopher. *The Responsibility Process: Unlocking Your Natural Ability to Live and Lead With Power* (2016)

Bogsnes, Bjarte. *Implementing Beyond Budgeting: Unlocking the Performance Potential*, 2nd edition (2016)

Brown, Brené. *Dare to Lead: Brave Work. Tough Conversations. Whole Hearts. (2018)*

Frahm, Klaus-Peter, Michael Schieben, and Wolfgang Wopperer-Beholz. *The Product Field Reference Guide (2016)*

Laloux, Frederic and Etienne Appert. *Reinventing Organizations: An Illustrated Invitation to Join the Conversation on Next-Stage Organizations* (2016)

Niven, Paul R. and Ben Lamorte. *Objectives and Key Results: Driving Focus, Alignment, and Engagement With OKRs* (2016)

O'Reilly, Barry. *Unlearn: Let Go of Past Success to Achieve Extraordinary Results* (2018)

Rosenberg, Marshall B. *Nonviolent Communication: A Language of Life: Life-Changing Tools for Healthy Relationships*, 3rd edition (2015)

Seiden, Joshua. *Outcomes Over Output. Why Customer Behavior Is the Key Metric for Business Success* (2019)

Thoren, Pia-Maria. *Agile People: A Radical Approach for HR & Managers* (2017)

ACKNOWLEDGMENTS

This book is not just the work of two people—it is the result of working and talking with many inspiring people and organizations around the globe, who shared their experiences, wanted to develop themselves further, and offered opinions, support and laughter. Thank you Mathias, Johannes, Andreas, Nermin, Iris, and all the others for your insights and reflections.

A big thank-you also goes to all the OKR evangelists—like John Doerr, Christina Wodtke, Felipe Castro, and many others—who share their knowledge as an open university in many interviews, books, articles. We are standing on your shoulders.

In particular, we would like to thank the Sense & Respond Press team for the opportunity to share our perspective on OKRs with the world. Thank you especially to Josh for supporting us in delivering the best book we could write today.

Thanks to all our friends who encouraged us during the process to make this possible. And last but absolutely not least thanks to Torsten and Tim, who supported us with their proofreading, love, presence, and understanding for many challenging months.

And finally a big thank-you to you as a reader for choosing to spend your time with our tips, conclusions, and reflections on OKRs. We hope you found what you were looking for and more—and we would appreciate your thoughts and feedback. If you would like to share your experiences and questions along your OKR journey with us, we are happy to hear from you via email (natalija@okrs-at-the-center.com or sonja@okrs-at-the-center.com) or to meet you through our global OKR practitioner community, https://www.meetup.com/OKR-Remote-English/.

NATALIJA HELLESOE is a trainer, coach and chance taker. She is keen on exploring new ways of working, living and learning and always striving to inspire people to redefine what is possible. Natalija has been working within People Development and Transformation since 2010 before starting her own business. Her work is shaped by living in and working with many different countries, cultures, and customers. She supports companies wanting to increase focus, autonomy, and value creation to prioritize their challenges and get started. She offers an entire ecosystem of training and coaching, focusing on Leadership & Responsibility, Agile HR, Remote Collaboration and Learning. Together with Sonja she also works with companies at different stages of their OKR journey—from first "Know-how" workshops to OKR Practitioner coaching and organizational development.

natalija@okrs-at-the-center.com
🐦 @natarctica
🔗 natalijahellesoe

SONJA MEWES is a consultant, trainer, and pattern seeker. Her personal objectives are to create connected and efficient collaboration—for people themselves and within their teams and organizations—to actively let them design their "beautiful future." Sonja has a diverse background in intercultural management, 10 years of multiple roles in the digital business industry, and last but not least in organizational development. She accompanies startups and corporations in experiencing, setting up, and developing new ways of collaboration, including OKRs and other approaches from nonviolent communication to remote working.

sonja@okrs-at-the-center.com
@sonja-mewes-960956b7
@beauti_future

Together, Natalija and Sonja strive to create a collaborative platform, in which OKR practitioners inside and outside of companies can explore the possibilities of developing organizations with OKRs (for more information, visit okrs-at-the-center.com).

Made in the USA
Monee, IL
24 November 2020